HIGHLIGHTS
FROM
FRANZ LEHARS

DIE LUSTIGE
WITWE

(THE MERRY WIDOW)

ORIGINAL GERMAN TEXT

Music Minus One

Franz Lehar's *Die Lustige Witwe (The Merry Widow)* was one of the greatest mega-hits in the history of operetta, and it quite possibly continues to hold to this day the record as the most frequently performed operetta of all time. Jaded as we are with multiple world-wide productions of such musicals as *My Fair Lady*, *Evita* and *The Phantom of the Opera*, we must not forget that a century ago *The Merry Widow* was the very first work to be performed around the world on such a massive scale. And this was long before the invention of radio, television, sound films and the long-playing record.

Die Lustige Witwe was first premièred on 30 December 1905 in the Hungarian Lehar's adopted city of Vienna, and shortly afterwards in Berlin, then in translation in Paris, London and New York. Within a few years of its début, the world knew that here was an unexpected phenomenon, a triumph of the operetta form not heard since the days of Offenbach and Johann Strauss II. Only a few of the works of Gilbert and Sullivan came remotely close to equaling this kind of popularity—but this was twenty years before.

If massive success of any performance-piece depends upon selling tickets to returning customers, then *Die Lustige Witwe* reigned supreme in its age. In every major city in Europe and the Americas, everyone sang and whistled its principal tunes and danced to its waltzes. And it was far ahead of its time in terms of mass-marketing, for here was possibly one of the first instances in which all sorts of unrelated objects such as hats, shoes, dresses, cigars, cookies, salads, puddings and biscuits suddenly flooded the market under the name "Merry Widow."

One year after its New York premiere, *The Merry Widow* had been performed more than 5,000 times in the United States alone. And in the multi-cultural city of Buenos Aires, five productions were playing simultaneously in five different languages. The work made Lehar an instant millionaire at thirty-five and put him on the map as the most popular composer of Vienna's last, glowing age of operetta. Certainly not since Johann Strauss's *Die Fledermaus* had anyone in Vienna composed an operetta that so captured the whole world by storm.

It's in *Die Lustige Witwe* and *Die Fledermaus* that we have twin perfect masterpieces of the lost but still much adored art of the operetta. Lehar was the undisputed musical heir to the younger Strauss, and both these masterpieces resemble one another in their unique abilities to blend nostalgia and sophisticated humor—while never departing from their joyously rapturous scores.

One is hard put to find anyone, from the most tone-deaf to the toughest enemy of the operetta form, who isn't swept off their feet by the rich melodies in *Die Lustige Witwe*. And rarely does one find any work with such a remarkable number of instantly hummable tunes.

—*Douglas Scharmann*

Music Minus One

MMO

4074

ORCHESTRAL BACKGROUNDS FOR

HIGHLIGHTS

FROM

FRANZ LEHARS

DIE LUSTIGE WITWE

(THE MERRY WIDOW)

LYRICS BY

VICTOR LEON AND LEO STEIN

Die Lustige Witwe

Synopsis

Act One

In Paris, the Pontevedrian ambassador to France, Baron Zeta, anxiously awaits the arrival at his Embassy of the recently widowed heiress Hanna Glawari. To prevent her fabulous fortune from leaving the impoverished Balkan state of Pontevedro, Baron Zeta decides he must prevent Hanna from marrying a foreigner.

After her arrival, Hanna is overwhelmed with attention from numerous Frenchmen who are interested in her solely for her wealth. She runs into a fellow countryman (and former lover from her youth), the playboy Count Danilo, who's just come from his favorite hang-out, Maxim's. Baron Zeta informs Danilo that for the sake of Pontevedro he must marry Hanna. But Danilo rejects this proposal, not wanting Hanna to think that, like the other men present, he is only courting her for her money.

The Baron becomes increasingly obsessed by this situation and fails to notice that his own wife Valencienne is on the brink of an affair with a young Frenchman, Camille de Rossillon. In the ballroom, Hanna chooses to dance with the one man who coldly ignores her, Count Danilo. He declines the offer, adding that if this dance belongs to him, he will bid it to charity for ten thousand francs.

Act Two

In order to make Count Danilo declare his love to her, Hanna gives a party in the garden of her villa. Entertainment is provided by dancers and singers in Pontevedrian costumes performing a national dance known as a "kolo." Hanna tells the guests a traditional national folk tale about a girl of the woods named "Vilja" and of a huntsman's unrequited love for her.

While Danilo and the men discuss the difficulties of dealing with women, it becomes apparent that he finds himself falling in love with Hanna all over again. Camille entices Valencienne into the garden's pavilion so that he may declare his passionate love for her. Baron Zeta peeks through the pavilion's keyhole, and spots Camille with a woman, which, to his horror, Zeta comes to think is his own wife.

Hanna comes to the rescue when she is quickly substituted for Valencienne as much to save her friend's reputation as to discovers Danilo's true feelings about her. In front of everyone, Camille repeats his declaration of love, but this time to Hanna, and she explains this surprising turn of events by announcing her engagement to Camille. Danilo is unable to conceal his disgust at this news and storms out. With this, Hanna knows for certain that he truly loves her.

Act Three

Hanna's villa is decked out as a cabaret spot and Valencienne performs a can-can with girls from Maxim's. Danilo seeks to forbid Hanna from marrying Camille, but he's shocked when she tells him her rendezvous in the pavilion with Camille was only a charade. The two can no longer disguise their love for each other and are together drawn into a sensuous waltz.

After Baron Zeta settles his problems with his wife, Hanna resorts to a stratagem to finally get Danilo to ask her to marry him—she announces she will lose her fortune upon her remarriage. At this news, Danilo asks for Hanna's hand. She agrees—and then explains that her millions will actually pass on to her next husband, after all.

—*Douglas Scharmann*

MMO 4074

ERSTER AKT.
Nº 1. Introduction.

6

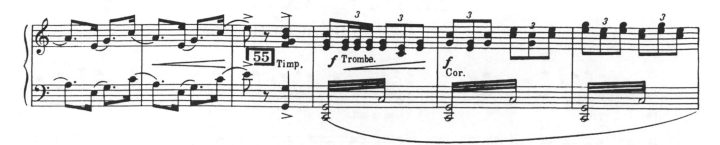

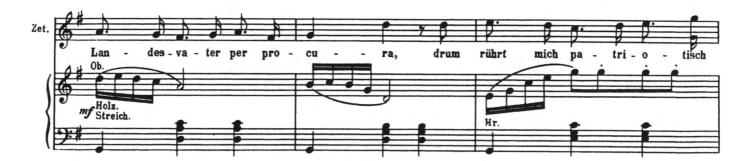

10

10

⊕ St. Brioche: Einen ruinierten Pariser? Wie nett!
⊕⊕ Zeta: Es ist ihr aber hübsch gewachsen, das Schnäbelchen!

Nᵒ 1½ Ballmusik.

⊕ Kromow: Nicht kokettieren! (ab mit Olga)
⊕⊕ Zeta: Es ist süss, fürs Vaterland zu erben! (ab.)

Nᵒ 2. Duett.
(Valencienne, Camille.)
(Ich bin eine anständ'ge Frau.)

12

14

16

Nᵒ 3. Entrée-Lied der Hanna und Ensemble.

⊕ Njegus: Um sich zu entschwipsen.
⊕⊕ Zeta: Melden Sie ihm sofort! das Vaterland ruft ihn!

Allegro.   (20 Herren, darunter Cascada und St. Brioche, eilen aus dem rückwärtigen Saale

über die Bühne, durch   Baron Zeta:(gesprochen:)Was hat denn das zu bedeuten? Cascada: Frau Glawari ist angekommen! (ab.)
die Haupttüre ab.)

St. Brioche: 20 Millionen! (rasch ab.)   Baron Zeta: Frau Glawari! (rasch ab.)   Njegus: Die lustige Witwe! Sie

trauert sehr fidel! Wenn ich nur einmal im Leben so viel Geld hätte, wie die — dann wär' ich auch ein lustiger Witwer!(ab.)   (Die Herren treten

wieder ein und bilden Spalier.)

Tempo di mazurka.

Hanna (zu den Herren, die sie umringen.)

Bit - te, mei - ne Herr'n!   Wel - che Ga - lant - rie'n...

Cascada.

Tempo di mazurka.   Sie sind der Ster - ne schön-ster Stern,   die hier strah - lend

(unterbricht ihn lachend.)
Han.
Bit - te, nicht doch! 'Sist ge - nug! Doch jetzt ge - en - det!
St. Brioche.
Und wie ein hol - der Sin - nen - trug, der uns blen - det...
Cas.
zieh'n...
Fl.
Harfe.
Han.
Hö - ren Sie! O bit - te, schweigen Sie! Sie machen mich ver - le - gen, mei - ne Herr'n!
St.B.
Empfangen Sie die Hul - di - gung als die - ses Fe - stes Stern! Als schön - ster Stern!
Cas.
Empfangen Sie die Hul - di - gung als die - ses Fe - stes Stern! Als schön - ster Stern!
Herren - Chor.
Empfangen Sie die Hul - di - gung als die - ses Fe - stes Stern! Als schön - ster Stern!
45
p Cello. Hfe.
Harfe.
p
50
rit.
Mazurka.
Han.
Hab' in Pa - ris mich noch nicht ganz so ac - cli - ma - ti - siert, dass die - ser sü - sse
Ob. u. 1. Vl.
pp
rit.
a tempo
Fl.
pp
1. Vl. mit Singst.
55
Harfe.
Han.
Fir - le - fanz von mir ver - stan - den wird! Bin noch Pon - te - ve -
60

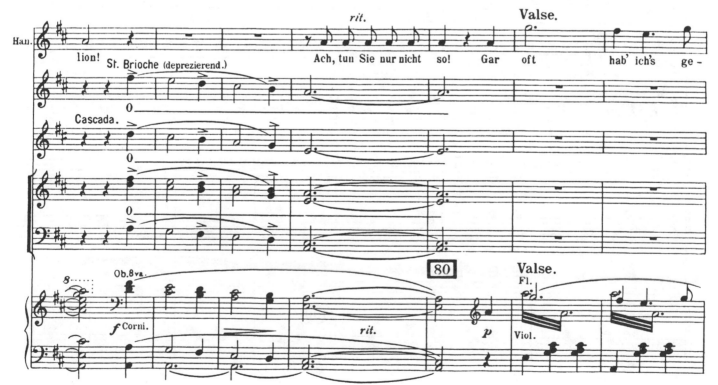

20

MMO 4074

22

Han. wird man auch fast nie-mals mo - le - stiert! Geht ei-ner gar in's Zeug so scharf,

St.B. macht Sie dop - pelt so rei - zend! Da -

Cas. macht Sie dop - pelt so rei - zend! Da -

macht Sie dop - pelt so rei - zend! Da -

125

Clar.

mf

Han. so un-ver-schämt wie Sie, dann weiss man wohl, dass er es darf, denn heu-cheln wird der

St.B. rum prei - se ich Sie voll Sym - pa -

Cas. rum prei - se ich Sie voll Sym - pa -

rum prei - se ich Sie voll Sym - pa -

130

Fl.

p

pp

MMO 4074

No. 4. Auftrittslied.
(Danilo.)

⊕ Hanna: Aber...So viele Arme.
⊕⊕ Valencienne: Unterstehn Sie sich! (ab mit Camille.)

Graf Danilo, harte slavische Aussprache tritt auf von Njegus begleitet.

Graf Danilo: Also bitte _ _ _ ich bin hier _ _ _ Wo ist das Vaterland?

Allegretto.

Njegus: Ich melde Sie sogleich Sr Excellenz.

Graf Danilo. Allegretto moderato.

O Va_ter_land du machst bei

Tutti.

Clar. Fag.

Tag mir schon ge _ nü _ gend Müh' und Plag! Die Nacht braucht je_der Di _ plo_

Viola

Corni

mat doch meistenteils für sich pri _ vat! Um Eins bin ich schon im Bu _ reau, doch bin ich

Fl.

Corni

Fl.

Clar. Fag.

26

gleich drauf an - ders - wo, weil man den gan - zen lie - ben Tag nicht im - mer

im Bu - reau sein mag! Kein Wun - der, wenn man so viel

thut, dass man am A - bend ger - ne ruht, und sich bei Nacht, was man so

nennt, Er - ho - lung nach der Ar - beit gönnt! Da geh' ich zu Ma - xim, dort

bin ich sehr in - tim, ich du - ze al - le Da - men, ruf' sie beim Ko - se -

MMO 4074

na - men, Lo - lo, Do - do, Jou - jou, Clo - clo, Mar - got, Frou - frou, sie las - sen mich ver -

ges - sen, das teu' - re Va - ter - land! Dann wird cham - pa - gni - siert, auch häu - fig can - ca -

niert, und geht's an's Ko - sen, Küs - sen mit al - len die - sen Süs - sen: Lo - lo, Do - do, Jou -

jou, Clo - clo, Mar - got, Frou - frou, dann kann ich leicht ver - ges - sen, das

teu' - re Va - ter - land.

from
№ 6. Finale I.

(Hanna, Valencienne, Danilo,
Camille, St. Brioche, Cascada, Chor.)

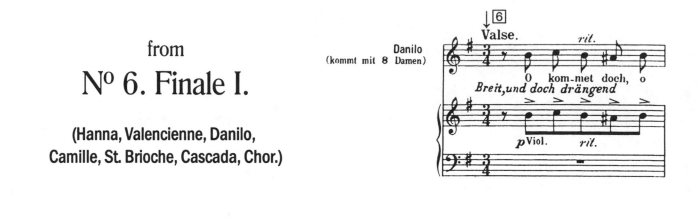

re - nen zö-gert nicht, das Fest zu krö-nen, seht da steht ein

1. Dame (knixt, zu dem jungen Mann) (die Beiden tanzen ab)

Tän - zer - heer! Al-so bit - te, bit - te sehr!

Danilo.

Wie die Blu - men im Len - ze er-blüh'n und in

Hanna.
O kom-met doch, o kommt, Ihr Ball-si - re - nen folgt den sü - ssen Wal-zer-

Danilo.
O kom-met doch, o kommt, Ihr Ball-si - re - nen folgt den sü - ssen Wal-zer-

St. Brioche.
O kom-met doch, o kommt, Ihr Ball-si - re - nen folgt den sü - ssen Wal-zer-

Cascada.
O kom-met doch, o kommt, Ihr Ball-si - re - nen folgt den sü - ssen Wal-zer-

Ach ja, wir fol-gen gern den sü - ssen Tö - nen, die das Le - ben uns ver-

O kom-met doch, o kommt, Ihr Ball-si - re - nen folgt den sü - ssen Wal-zer-

streng im tempo *f Tutti.*

Han.
tö - nen wie sie sin-gen und klin-gen, o tanzt doch mit, hebt Eu - re Füss-chen ein

Dan.
tö - nen wie sie sin-gen und klin-gen, o tanzt doch mit, hebt Eu - re Füss-chen ein

St. B.
tö - nen wie sie sin-gen und klin-gen, o tanzt doch mit, hebt Eu - re Füss-chen ein

Cas.
tö - nen wie sie sin-gen und klin-gen, o tanzt doch mit, hebt Eu - re Füss-chen ein

schö - nen wie sie sin-gen und klin-gen, o Wal-zer-schritt, wirst uns be - sie-gen, wir

tö - nen wie sie sin-gen und klin-gen, o tanzt doch mit, hebt Eu - re Füss-chen ein

(Alles tanzt ab bis auf: Hanna, Danilo, St. Brioche, Cascada und 4 Herren.)

klingt, tanzt leicht be - schwingt!

klingt, tanzt leicht be - schwingt!

klingt, tanzt leicht be - schwingt!

klingt, tanzt leicht be - schwingt!

schwingt, so lang er - klingt!

klingt, so lang er - klingt!

Valse moderato.

(Er steht hinter ihr, versucht, ihr in's Gesicht zu sehen, sie wendet den Kopf kokett immer weg.)

34

Hanna (kämpft)   (kämpft noch eine Weile, fliegt unwillkürlich in seine Arme und tanzt mit ihm.)

Nein ich will nicht! (Er tanzt allein um sie herum.)

streng im Walzertempo

a tempo   *p* —— *mf con tenerezza*   *poco a poco cresc.*

Han.   (schon tanzend.)   Danilo.

Sie ab - scheu-li-cher Mann!   Wie prächtig Sie tan - zen!   Man

mf

Dan.   thut was man kann!

mf   *a. f*   Tutti *ff*   (Vorhang ab.)

(Sie tanzen Beide ab)

sempre più forte et molto animato

Presto.

fff   *ff*   *ff*   *ff*   *ff*

from
ZWEITER AKT.
№ 7. Introduktion, Tanz und Vilja-Lied.
(Lied vom Waldmägdelein.)

(Hanna, Chor.)

40

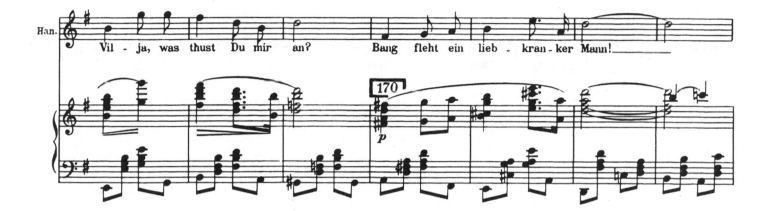

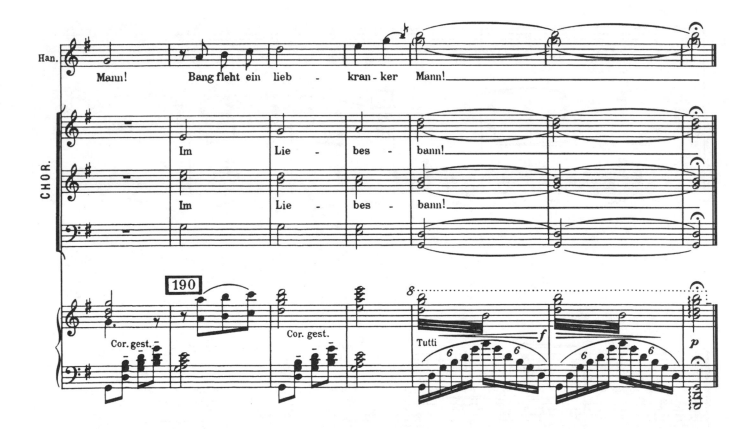

№ 9. Marsch-Septett.

(Danilo, Zeta, Cascada, St. Brioche, Kromow, Bogdanowitsch, Pritschitsch.)

Kromow: Ich mache den Lumpen eiskalt.
Zeta: Darüber brauche ich, Gott sei Dank, nicht nachzudenken.

44

MMO 4074

48

50

MMO 4074

52

54

* Bei eventueller Wiederholung die 2. Strophe (im Textbuch enthalten) zu singen.

Nº 10 Spielszene und Tanzduett.
(Hanna, Danilo.)

✦ Hanna. Ob ich den heiraten soll den ich möchte.
✦✦ Danilo. Sie brauchen sich also nichts einzubilden.

Hanna: (auf ihn zustürzend) Sie sind... Danilo: Was? Hanna: Sie sind... Danilo: Was? (Hanna, wendet sich ärgerlich ab.) Danilo kämpft mit sich, will sie ansprechen, wendet sich aber trotzig ab, geht gegen den Hintergrund und bleibt dort, ihr den Rücken zuwendend stehen. Musik beginnt. (Hanna erblickt den Fächer) Hanna (sprechend): Ein Damenfächer u. s. w.

Hanna. Avec beaucoup de plaisir, cher Baron
Danilo. Un Kolo, la danse de notre patrie!

II. Allegretto moderato.

Hanna: Sehen Sie, da würde ich zu meinem Manne sagen: Lieber Da..!Danilo.(freudig) Da? Hanna (lacht) Dagobert!Desswe-

58

I. mal: Danilo. Es kommt gleich
ein anderer, der
tanzt auch gut.

II. mal: Hanna: Was thut man
dort? Danilo: Man tanzt auch
nur bissel auf andere Weise.

№ 11. Duett und Romanze.

(Valencienne, Camille.)

Camille: So geben Sie mir doch wenigstens ein Andenken.
Camille: Jetzt hab ichs schriftlich. Valencienne!

Val. Sie wolln mich doch nicht kom-pro-mi - tie - ren?

Cam. im - mer Dich ver - lie - ren? Das will ich

animato

Val. So ist es recht, so hab' ich Dich lieb.

Cam. nicht! Das darf ich nicht! (glühend) Ich

(wehrt ihn ab)

Val. Sie ma - chen mich bö - se!

Cam. muss Dich küs - sen. Ver - gib! Ver - gib! Mein Lieb!

Romanze.
Allegretto.

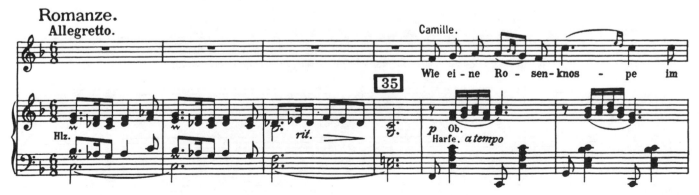

Camille.

Wie ei - ne Ro - sen - knos - pe im

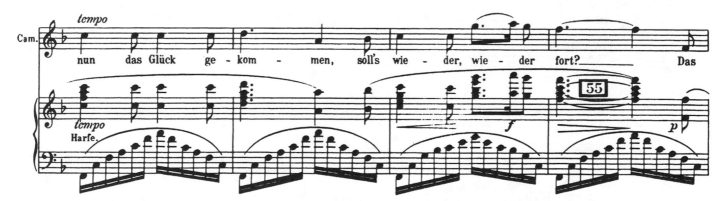

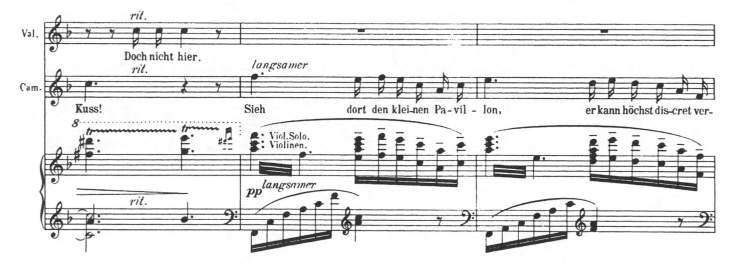

64

DRITTER AKT.
№ 12ᵇ Zwischenspiel.

Beim Aufziehen des Vorhanges setzt die Musik hinter der Scene ein.
(Bühnenmusik ad lib.)

Allegretto.

Sobald das Orchester mit dem Cake Walk einsetzt, unterbricht die Bühnencapelle ihr
Spiel und spielt den Cake Walk mit.

№ 13. Tanz=Szene.

✛ Njegur: Eine Weltdame halbiert sich oft über Nacht!
✛✛ Zeta: Also los!

Tempo di marcia. (Cake Walk.)　(Die Bühnenmusik spielt mit.)

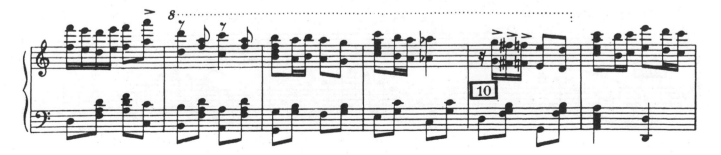

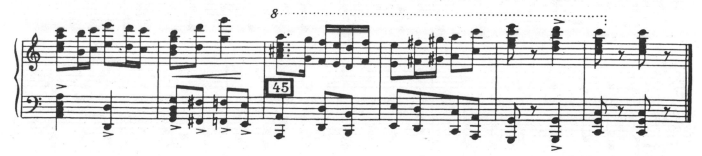

✢ Die nächste Nummer schliesst sich sofort an.

MMO 4074

from
Nº 14. Chanson.
Grisetten-Lied.

(Valencienne, Lolo, Dodo, Jou-Jou, Frou-Frou, Clo-Clo, Margot, Danilo, Zeta, Bogdanowitsch, Pritschitsch, Kromow, Chor.)

70

MMO 4074

from the English-language version:

Nº 14b. Butterflies

74

CHORUS IN UNISON.

CHO.

1. We are the dear lit-tle but-ter-flies that hov-er
2. Plen-ty of men try to cap-ture us and net us.

p 2nd *f*

CHO.

All a-round a lov-er, And for beau-ty none can match us!
No-bo-dy can get us, We are ve-ry hard to cap-ture!

CHO.

We flut-ter by you up-on a breeze of laugh-ter
Pray try a-gain and you will not al-ways miss us.

CHO.

1.
Won't you come af-ter Us and catch us!
2.
If you should kiss us. Oh, what rap ture!

DANCE.

accel: *poco*   *a*   *poco*   *al* *fine*

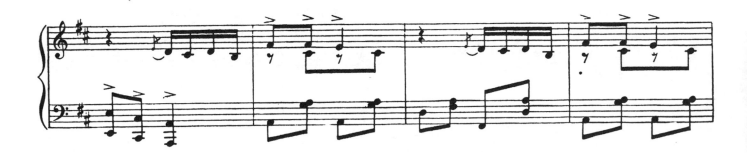

№ 15. Duett.
Lippen schweigen.
(Hanna, Danilo.)

⊕ Hanna: So machen Sie doch den Mund auf.

⊕⊕ Danilo: So bin ich ganz wo anders zu Hause. (Musik beginnt)

Valse moderato.

Danilo: Aber dort bin ich zu Hause.   Hanna: (auf ihn zugehend) O Sie sind.....

Danilo: (herausfordernd) Was bin ich? (Hanna wendet sich ab.) Danilo: O Du bist.... Hanna: (hoffend, dass er ein liebes Wort sagt)

Was bin ich? (Beide verstummen. Hanna blickt sinnend in die Ferne und setzt sich zum Tisch. Danilo kämpft mit seinen Gefühlen) Danilo.

Lip - pen schwei - gen, 's flü - stern Gei - gen: Hab'

Dan.

mich lieb! All' die Schrit - te sa - gen bit - te, hab'

Dan.

mich lieb! Je - der Druck der Hän - de deut - lich

MMO 4074

Dan. mir's be - schrieb_____ Er sagt klar 's ist wahr, 's ist wahr, du

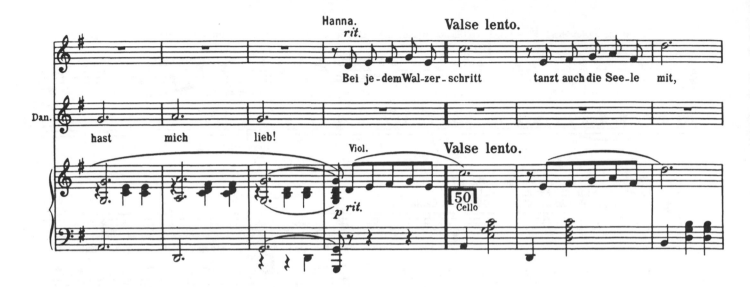

Hanna. rit. Valse lento.

Bei je - dem Wal-zer - schritt tanzt auch die See - le mit,

Dan. hast mich lieb!

Viol. Valse lento.

Han. da hüpft das Herz chen klein es klopft und pocht: Sei mein! Sei mein! Und der Mund er spricht kein Wort

leise flüsternd

pp

Han. doch tönt es fort und im-mer-fort: Ich hab' dich ja so lieb, ich hab' dich lieb!_____

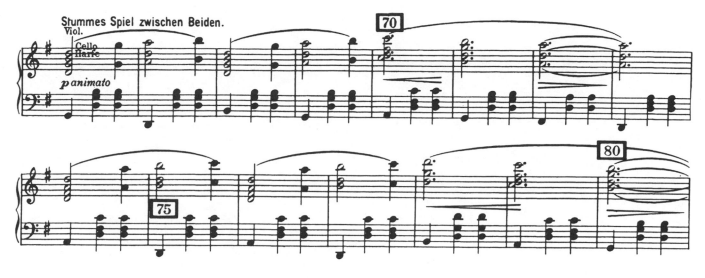

MUSIC MINUS ONE
50 Executive Boulevard
Elmsford, New York 10523-1325
800-669-7464 (U.S.)/914-592-1188 (International)

www.musicminusone.com
e-mail: mmomusicgroup@musicminusone.com

MMO 4074